"Thought-provoking, moving and often profound, these daily "you moments" are the perfect way to jumpstart your day or just be inspired anytime. Keri Nola gets right to the point and gives us succinct reminders to own up to our worthiness and embrace the power of our choices. I love it!"

~Paula Renaye, Award-Winning Author, Living the Life You Love--
The No-Nonsense Guide to Total Transformation

"Delightfully empowering...Keri Nola has outdone herself with this inspiring compilation of daily affirmations. Chock-full of positive energy, they speak directly to our soul and motivate us to move forward and take charge of our lives."

~Sherri Cortland, author, Windows of Opportunity and Raising
Our Vibrations for the New Age

"Keri Nola's debut book is ultimately about connecting to our souls, and thus returning to the love that we are. She shines the light on this process through a thought provoking and inspiring collection of her daily bits of wisdom and expertise. A Year on Your Path to Growth leads us further on our journey to self love, which directly helps us to create a much more loving and peaceful world."

~Mary Soliel, Award- Winning author of I Can See Clearly Now
and Michael's Clarion Call

"Keri's lovely book is filled with daily gems of inspiration that will raise your vibration and expand your awareness. With Keri as your guide, you can actually feel her lovingly cheering you on, inviting you to discover and embrace your authentic, radiant Self. This is a must read for anyone who is ready to awaken to their Power and Presence as a loving expression of the Divine."

~Jill Lebeau, MFT, coauthor of Feng Shui Your Mind, Four Easy
Steps to Rapidly Transform Your Life!

D1082066

A Year on Your Path To Growth

Daily Inspirations to Reconnect With Your Soul

Keri Nola

BALBOA
PRESS
A DIVISION OF HAY HOUSE

Cover and interior photos and interior layout and design by: Monica Alfonso
Edited by: Jonathan Hiett

Balboa Press books may be ordered through booksellers or by contacting:

Balboa Press
A Division of Hay House
1663 Liberty Drive
Bloomington, IN 47403
www.balboapress.com
1-(877) 407-4847

Printed in the United States of America

ISBN: 978-1-4525-5382-5 (sc)
ISBN: 978-1-4525-5383-2 (hc)
ISBN: 978-1-4525-5381-8 (e)

Library of Congress Control Number: 2012910959
Balboa Press rev. date: 6/28/2012

Acknowledgments

To my ancestors...thank you for coming before me and paving the way for my earth journey; I continue to feel your inspiration and love from beyond the veil, and I honor you.

To my Mother, Father, and sister...you were my first and most influential teachers on my path to growth, and our relationships have inspired the birth of this book; I am infinitely grateful for your love.

To Jayden and Tamia...loving you has opened my heart in ways I never imagined possible. I am forever changed by your presence, which is one of my life's most treasured blessings.

To Angela, Casandra, J, and the other healers and spiritual teachers who have and continue to hold space for me to integrate the wounded parts of myself...thank you for seeing and loving me as I learned to love myself. You have each helped me find the courage to birth this book into being.

To Chonteau...the sisterhood we have created revitalizes my soul! Thank you for taking a leap of faith in cultivating our friendship, which has evolved into one of my life's greatest gifts.

To Cory...from Crazyville and back again, you meet me wherever I am and love me right through it...thank you for always being a gentle mirror for me to get real to heal.

To Jennifer…your unconditional love brings me back home to my most authentic self. Thank you for loving me even when I talk in the pitch only dogs can hear.

To Jonathan…your intuition, keen eyes, and brilliant editing skills transformed my vision for this book into a readable piece of art. Thank you for the mindful, delicate care you took in your role of editor.

To Monica…your creative vision inspired the completion of this book. Thank you for capturing the essence of my words in your Divine photography and for your endless hours of shooting and editing; your labor helped to birth my dream into reality, and I am forever grateful for this gift you've given me.

To Sherri…you were the seasoned author I turned to for support and guidance as I navigated the ropes of being a first time author. Thank you for your generous responses to my excessive emails, for connecting me with other talented authors who are also becoming friends, and mostly for celebrating with me each step of the way.

To my Balboa Press team…Mollie, Jennifer, Brian, designers, and everyone else behind the scenes..thank you for your mindful expertise and professionalism in guiding my publishing process and being the final hands in making my vision of this book a reality. I am full of gratitude!

And to all the souls I have and do call "friends"…thank you for the many ways you enrich my life. Our connections have been deeply meaningful on my journey and have ultimately inspired me to discover my authentic self and the lessons I share in this book.

To all of the courageous souls who have allowed me to hold a sacred space for their healing—my past, present, and future clients...it will always be my privilege to witness a piece of your path to growth.

Contents

Preface

I unknowingly began writing this book in January 2010 when I decided to take a leap out of my comfort zone and create a Facebook Fan page for my integrative healing practice, Path To Growth, LLC. I began posting daily inspirations and at that time did not consciously create any common threads running through the posts; it was simply a mirror of lessons I was working on in my own life. From time to time, fans suggested that I compile the posts into a book and while I was flattered by the encouragement and belief in my material, the idea didn't resonate with me for some time (translation: I was scared to death!).

Fast forward to January 2011 when I was on a three-hour drive back home from an evening with Dr. Wayne Dyer where he spoke of the art of manifestation. I found myself meditating on the idea of publishing a book. I could feel a passion rise up from within me, and I found myself experiencing a moment of pure bliss, which told me this was a heart-inspired vision. Then fear crept in, and I heard my inner critic say, "What do you know that you think the world would want to hear?" In that moment, I tried to locate my highest self, who I desperately hoped would know the answer to what seemed to be a reasonable question, and there was silence. Instead of letting the fear and doubt take over, something within me said, "Just breathe into the silence." And so with tears streaming down my cheeks, I took a deep breath and waited for a brilliant answer… nothing. I took another deep breath and…nothing! By this time (all 15 seconds!), I thought "Oh no, I've lost my highest self! Where could she have gone?" Then on the third breath, I heard, "You've already written the book. You've been writing it every day for the past year." Whew! There she is…that was a close call. "Thought I lost you there for a minute," I said to myself. Feeling confused about what my inner wisdom was referring to,

I sat for a moment and thought about what it could mean. My Facebook page and its daily affirmations then floated into mind...I had already birthed the book. I now just needed to find the courage to nurture and love it into publication, and as you can see, since you're holding it in your hands, I did.

Guide to using this book:

My hope for all readers of this book is that you will personalize its possibilities to meet your unique needs at the time you pick it up. There is no "right" way to move on your path...there's just YOUR way. For some, you may choose to start at the beginning and go day by day like a calendar. For others it may make more sense to choose a chapter with a theme that resonates with you at this time in your life. Or perhaps sometimes to open up to a random page when you need a burst of inspiration is its best use. I invite you to honor yourself as you continue your journey and know that I am on it with you...

May these words connect us all to a deep knowing of our Divine right to infinite peace, love, and prosperity on our path to growth.

Infinite Blessings of Light and Love,
Keri

Chapter 1

You're Worth It!

Now more than ever we are being called to assist in raising the vibration of our planet by moving through layer upon layer of experiences that have led us to falsely question our worth and lovability. Contrary to popular belief, love and worth are not realities we earn; rather, they are Divine rights that belong to us simply because we were born. The truth is that we have always been worthy and lovable, friends...now we're just working to remember these truths.

Instead of getting yourself caught in the web of "not enough" and attempting to measure your worth by progress on your New Year's "resolutions", this month I invite you to journey inside and discover what you have been telling yourself about the story of your unworthiness and lack of lovability and learn ways to shift into the truth of your Divine brilliance!

January 1

Today is the day to remember your magnificence and stand in it proudly! You are not here to shrink down and pretend you are unworthy, unlovable, or less than others…you are here to shine brightly and let your gifts benefit the planet at this important time. Where have you forgotten your magnificence and Divine perfection? What is one thing you can do today to step back into it?

January 2

What if you allowed yourself to be "good enough" at this very moment? That doesn't mean, "I'll be good enough when I lose more weight, get a new job, am in a relationship, am a better parent, etc." It means stop in this very moment, take a deep breath, and declare from the deepest, wisest part of yourself, "I AM good enough right now."

January 3

It is your birthright to experience Joy. Pay attention to the stories you may have created to talk yourself out of feeling joyous. Pay attention to the ways your ego tries to convince you that you're different from others and that you don't deserve the happiness that you see others experiencing. Smile today and know that you can just because you're alive and you deserve to feel Joy!

January 4

Allow yourself to take up space today. How often do you shrink yourself down so as not be noticed or considered arrogant? How often do you consider yourself "not enough" in the presence of others? Each day is a new opportunity to step into yourself and claim your space and your right to be in it...just for today, stand a little taller and walk a little prouder as you celebrate being YOU.

January 5

Speak up! How can you give yourself permission to stop apologizing for who you are and start speaking up so your valuable voice can be heard? Today, consider what you have to say and give yourself permission to share it with the world!

January 6

What are you looking for? If you want proof that you don't deserve this or that, you can always find it. Why not look for all the reasons you deserve incredible joy, peace, love, and prosperity? Today, find proof for that too!

January 7

Saying "No" to others often means saying "Yes" to yourself. Is it time to say "Yes!" to yourself more often? Keep in mind that this practice keeps our relationships honest and prevents resentments from building. Consider where you have been saying "Yes" when you have really meant "No" and allow yourself to change that up today—you're worth it!

<u>J</u>anuary 8

Contrary to popular belief, we don't bend over backwards
doing for other people out of the goodness of our hearts.
These people- pleasing behaviors are often driven by
our attempts to feel needed, wanted, appreciated, and
worthy. The evidence of this reality shows up in feelings
of resentfulness, bitterness, and anger in our relationships.
Just for today may you recognize where you are hustling for
your worth, allow yourself to set aside the measuring stick,
and acknowledge your unlimited worth even though…

January 9

It does not matter what you did yesterday or the day before yesterday. Today is a new and fresh opportunity, and you can decide again. May you decide something that welcomes the incredible joy and abundance you deserve!

January 10

What would life be like if you chose to do only the things that you wanted to do with those whom you wanted to do them with? Notice any defensiveness and resistance to this thought.

Before you come up with all the ways this couldn't be your reality, think about it for a moment…what would life look like if you said "No, thank you" to that which doesn't resonate with you? It is your birthright to live the life you want, and it is your job to make that happen. There's no day but today…go for it!

January 11

You're worthy. If there seems to be any confusion, let's clear it up now…YOU were born worthy. This worth and value is beyond anything you could ever fathom, and there are no experiences or lack thereof that may happen in life that can add to or deplete your worth. So rest assured that whether your humanly mistakes add up to one million or zero, your worth will remain the same…Infinite! Now breathe that in…

January 12

No matter what you've done or haven't done, what you do or do not do, and what has or has not been done to you, the truth is that your lovability has never changed. You are lovable beyond your wildest imagination!

January 13

How long do you force yourself to pay for something that you are ashamed of doing, saying, or being? Humanness is a perfectly imperfect journey, and yet we often hold ourselves to unattainable standards. What would it be like for you to forgive yourself and acknowledge your right to happiness now? No one else is going to do it for you...it's up to you.

January 14

Are you looking for the buoys or the obstacles in your life? Sometimes lifelines are disguised as struggles, and it's your responsibility to choose how you will see your reality to move forward peacefully. You are being supported right now. Look around and discover that truth in your life today.

January 15

Take an inventory of your choices today. Are you making choices that do not resonate with your highest self? If so, get curious about a part of you that may be feeling undeserving of love, peace, abundance, and joy and see if you can give that part of you some of your attention and recognition.

January 16

When we remember our worth, we choose ourselves without guilt or shame. How can you choose yourself today?

January 17

Life isn't about running and rushing to do more and more. No one's last words have been, "I wish I worked more, cleaned more, or cooked more." Life is about discovering our passion, creating, loving, and experiencing joy and peace. What can you do today with the intention of being less "perfect" and instead more "happy?" Be the boss of your happiness today…now this is a job worth having!

January 18

Do you ever visit the "Crazy Place?" You know, the imaginary destination in your mind where you create the story that you are unworthy of love and compassion, where your world is an unforgiving and judgmental place and you are all alone? Doesn't sound too pleasant, does it? Today, revoke your residency in Crazyville and come back to the reality of your worthiness, where you create a joyful and loving experience for yourself!

January 19

Show up for yourself today. Be present in your experiences, gently acknowledge your reactions to those experiences, and give yourself permission to make mistakes and grow through them. Lower the bar from expectations of perfection to a loving awareness of your humanness and know that you are perfect and worthy even though…

January 20

What is it like for you to receive compliments? This doesn't mean just hearing one; it means welcoming it without justification or excuse and simply being able to mindfully say, "Thank you." Sometimes someone offers us a genuine compliment and parts of us disagree with that we've heard, and we start giving a litany of reasons why that person is wrong. Just for today, see if you can create a category within yourself called "Compliments" and welcome them gracefully in.

<u>January 21</u>

Take a moment and discover what you've been holding back, and give yourself and the world the gift of showing up fully today. When we grasp the totality of our worth, we stand tall and allow our gifts to overflow. What are you allowing to block your brilliant light from shining upon?

January 22

Our evolution is a gradual process that unfolds with love, patience, and time. Just for today, choose a change you'd like to make and commit to practicing one action in the direction of the experience you desire. Then acknowledge your efforts each step of the way; celebration is an equally important part of the transformation journey. Remember to celebrate YOU!

January 23

View what you do today as an opportunity to create. Whether it's a report at the office or an experience with a loved one, feel your passion in the process of creating and know that you are capable of producing miracles!

January 24

When we release others from the role of responsibility for our worth, we are free to love them and ourselves unconditionally. Who are you still making responsible for determining your worthiness?

January 25

As soon as we realize our worth, we stop allowing ourselves to be controlled by the opinions and thoughts of others. What experience are you still allowing to deem you unworthy, and how can you gently release your grip on that story and free yourself today?

January 26

Simply because you were born, you are enough.

Say this out loud…"Simply because I was born, I am enough."

If you notice resistance to this statement, try starting with an in-process affirmation such as, "I am willing to consider that simply because I was born, I am enough."

January 27

When we find ourselves staying at jobs we don't like or in relationships that are abusive, it's because we don't believe we're worthy of anything better. Ask yourself today, "Where am I settling for less than I deserve?

January 28

Abundance is your birthright. Abundant health,
abundant peace, abundant love, and abundant wealth…
if you find yourself feeling stuck in lack, this is an issue
of worthiness. If you knew you were worthy, what would
you be allowing to exist in your life right now?

January 29

Societies and cultures often communicate to us that
we have to be more and do more to earn our worth…
get another degree, achieve a promotion, get married, be
skinnier, be more muscular. All these messages relate to
something other than what we are as being acceptable.
For today, examine what unconscious messages may be
impacting your actions. Can you fathom that you'd be
enough even if you didn't "achieve" one more thing?

January 30

Peace is your birthright. Have you created a story that there is a person or experience keeping you from peace? Creating stories that others have the power to keep us from peace leaves us powerless. Decide today that no matter what you've experienced, you can process it, heal the wound, and experience the peace you deserve. Re-empower yourself today!

January 31

Welcome home to your worthiness…it's always been here…
where have you been? Today you're invited to remember
that if you're feeling unworthy, undeserving, or unlovable,
you're the one that's changed because this fact never has:
YOU, my friend, are worthy and lovable beyond your wildest
imagination…always have been and always will be! Now
pause and breathe that in for a moment…ahhhhhh

Chapter 2

Wrap Yourself In Love

The most important relationship we will ever cultivate is the one we have with ourselves. Attachment theory research tells us that the way we learn how to relate to ourselves is by witnessing and experiencing the love from our caretakers to us, from our caretakers to themselves, and between our caretakers. Even with the best intentions, our parents or other adult caretakers often have unhealed aspects of themselves that keep them from being able to fully connect and engage with us as children in ways that help us learn the important skill of self-love. If you are a parent or have children in your life, one of the greatest gifts you can give them is to intentionally heal your own emotional wounds and learn how to love and care for yourself because it is from their witnessing this process that those children will grow up to be able to mimic it for themselves.

This chapter will gently guide you to an awareness of where you may be emotionally abandoning and neglecting yourself and will offer you ways to establish a solid foundation of self-love that will support you through the peaks and valleys of your human experience. May you give yourself permission to read along and commit to engaging mindfully in a journey of learning how to love yourself fully and completely without apology.

<u>February 1</u>

We all want to be loved, we want to feel like we belong, and we want to know that we matter. Just for today, will you remind yourself that you are loved, you belong, and you matter?

February 2

What part of yourself have you been denying or ignoring lately? All parts of you are valuable and have helped you to survive different times in your life. If you're finding that the behavior of a part of yourself is no longer necessary, consider building a relationship with this part of you; it's working *with* instead of against ourselves that allows for change.

February 3

Mother Nature doesn't judge herself when she's gloomy, so why do we? How about today you allow yourself to honestly reflect the state you're in, whether that be sunny, cloudy, rainy, snowy, or stormy? The weather is always more tolerable when we accept it for what it is and dress accordingly. Here's to meeting yourself where you are without judgment today!

February 4

When we get honest with ourselves about our history, our patterns, and our behaviors, it's easy to judge these truths as "good" or "bad," which can then translate into labeling ourselves as "good" or "bad." Today, try viewing your truths with curiosity; notice the feelings the truth reveals, and then hold them with compassion so that it can heal.

February 5

How can you elevate yourself to a place of peace and love today? Close your eyes for a moment and take in a deep breath. Envision a peaceful and loving experience and allow the vibration you are tuned into to invite more in.

February 6

How many times in life have you been told to "Be Quiet," "Be Still," Be good," or essentially BE something other than what you are in any given moment. Today, bring awareness to the messages you are repeating to yourself and see if you can allow yourself to make some noise! Laugh when something is funny, cry when you feel the urge, speak up when it is time to establish a boundary or share an idea…let your spirit out of the closet!

February 7

Fall in love with yourself today! Think about what you love more about yourself today than you were able to yesterday and consider what you hope to love more about yourself tomorrow than you do today. Here's to a day filled with all the self-love you can imagine!

February 8

Judge-Mental. When we judge, we are affected mentally, emotionally, and spiritually. Today, consider where you are judging yourself and see where you can welcome more gentleness. It's one thing to take accountability for your behaviors and another to continually beat yourself up.

February 9

What would life be like if you took responsibility for your own happiness and made decisions that honored your heart? The most loving gift you can give yourself and others is to relinquish your loved ones from the impossible job of making you happy and start loving yourself enough to make you happy! Dare you start today?

February 10

We spend a lot of time trying to fill our feelings of emptiness with the external…people, work, sex, shopping, substances, hobbies… and then we're surprised when we still don't feel full. Today consider how you can fill yourself from the inside out so the results can last longer. Your power lies in this kind of responsibility for yourself.

February 11

Others may think we are the most amazing person on the planet, but the truth is it doesn't really matter what they think because if we don't believe it first, it will be hard for us to believe them. For today, can you admit the truth of how amazing you are?

February 12

Loving others doesn't mean determining what's best for them. When we become the judge of others, we abandon ourselves. For today, when you notice yourself being the authority on others and what they should or shouldn't be doing, gently re-direct your focus back home to you. After all, that's the only place you have any authority.

<u>February 13</u>

Truly taking care of ourselves means not waiting for others to anticipate our needs and say or do "nicer" things for us. Today is the perfect day to get to work in anticipating and meeting your own needs and doing/ saying nice things to yourself! Ready, set, go!

February 14

What or who can you love more today than you did yesterday, and how can your behavior be congruent with this truth? While your first thought may be about someone or something outside of yourself, the opportunity may lie within you. What can you love more about yourself today, and how can you let your actions demonstrate that? Go ahead! Love the heck out of yourself today!

February 15

Most of us have heard the saying, "Do unto others as you'd have them do unto you," right? Well the problem isn't just in how we treat others, but how we treat ourselves too, so today, try this variation on for size…"Do unto YOURSELF as you would do unto others." No more excuses for treating yourself harshly! Will you let love in today?

February 16

We are often quick to run to the rescue when a friend calls us in crisis, but how quickly do we show up for ourselves when we are in need? Tune into your body, mind, and spirit today and hear the call of your soul. Your Divine self within is full of wisdom and answers when you just ask and listen.

February 17

Today, give yourself permission to just be. You don't need to be "fixed" or "changed"...one of life's greatest lessons of the human experience is discovering how we can meet ourselves where we are in all the cycles and rhythms of this thing called "life." No matter where you are today, can you commit to meeting yourself there in kindness and love?

February 18

When we love others more than we love ourselves, we are willing to settle for less than we deserve. Instead of wishing you were thinner, richer, better looking, whatever"er," see if you can shift your focus onto your favorite things about yourself. For today, give yourself permission to fall in love with you!

February 19

We all have parts of ourselves that feel a desperate need for acceptance and love. For today, instead of shaming the part of you that craves love and attention, see if you can sit with it for a moment and hold it in love. Ahhhhh...

<u>February 20</u>

How much time do you spend comparing and contrasting
yourself with others, rating if you are better or worse,
and then feeling accordingly? Today is the perfect day
to recognize that pattern, begin to acknowledge your
uniqueness, and honor yourself for being just who you are.

February 21

Be gentle with yourself as old patterns revisit. When old ways of thinking or behaving make a surprise visit, instead of judging yourself for taking two steps back, see if you can get curious about the value of this return to this place and allow these patterns to show you where you can still experience healing. Here's to loving yourself even though...

February 22

What part of yourself have you been refusing to love?
Allow yourself to honestly acknowledge where you
have been refusing yourself care and compassion and
give yourself permission to recommit to consciously
falling in love with this part of you today.

February 23

So often we are desperate for others to love and approve of us because we are struggling to take accountability for this job ourselves. When you love and approve of yourself, you feel less concerned about what others think of you, and you experience a kind of freedom from a painful mental prison. How about it? Are you ready to show up for the most important job you'll ever accept...loving you?

<u>February 24</u>

Reflect on your progress today. What hurdles have you overcome that you haven't yet given yourself credit for? What are you looking at differently in your life that has freed you from self-judgment and shame? What can you do to celebrate all that you have accomplished thus far? It's all about YOU... celebrate your successes, no matter how big or small they may seem, as they are the stepping stones that move you forward!

February 25

Love yourself unconditionally today. It's hard to welcome unconditional love from others when we don't have that experience internally first. Since our relationships are mirror images, if you are seeing and experiencing what feels like "conditional" love in relationships, let that remind you of the opportunity to love yourself without condition. Here's to continued learning about loving yourself even though...

February 26

You are a multi-dimensional being capable of holding
contradictory feelings and thoughts at the same time.
Instead of judging your contradictions today, give yourself
permission to sit with them and love yourself anyway!

February 27

Sometimes it's tempting to lose ourselves in an "us" or in the feelings of the lack of an "us." The greatest gift you can give yourself and your present or future partners is showing up whole because you committed to loving yourself. So today, celebrate YOU and remind yourself how incredibly lovable you are!

February 28

What if you chose to love yourself *even though* today? Even though you're sad, angry, scared, or joyful...even though the house is a mess, the laundry isn't done, a deadline got missed, you have a stain on your shirt...even though you have yet to break a habit, pattern, or relationship dynamic you've been struggling with...wherever you are today, may you choose to meet yourself there with gentleness and love.

Chapter 3

Feel Your Way Into Spring

Feelings…the best and the worst thing in life, right? They are what we long to experience and yet what we also fear the most. Often times we learn very young that a broad range of human emotion is not tolerated well in our families. For some, only joy is allowed, for others anger is prominent, and for others, expressions of sadness are forbidden. Whether communicated to us directly or covertly, as children we discover what is acceptable, and to survive, we repress the rest. Today, as adults it is our job to reconnect with that which we have denied so that we can now experience the fullness of our lives. The truth is we cannot numb the "unwanted" feelings like shame, sadness, and fear and still access the full range of desirable feelings such as peace, love, and joy. If we are ready for joy, we must allow ourselves to feel our way through the pain. This month we journey into the world of feeling and explore how we can meet ourselves with compassion in each moment, acknowledge the feeling there, and transcend it so we can know peace.

March 1

You know the worst thing that could ever happen to you? Feelings. Think about it for a moment…we don't want to set boundaries in our relationships because we FEEL afraid of people's reactions and our own. We stay in relationships that don't resonate with us because we don't want to FEEL the grief of leaving. We try to control our loved ones because we don't want to FEEL alone, unlovable, or rejected…the list goes on and on. Your life will shift in dramatic ways when you start to acknowledge and allow your authentic feelings with compassion instead of going against the tide and resisting them. How can you get real to heal about any feelings you've been avoiding and love yourself while you let them flow today?

March 2

Today, ask yourself, "If I weren't afraid, what would I do?"
Your answer will lead you to your truth, and you can recognize
your power to acknowledge the fearful part of you with
compassion so you can move forward when the time is right.

March 3

When we don't feel fulfilled, we are willing to "plug in" to all kinds of things to help distract us from this discomfort: overworking, unhealthy relationships, risky habits, etc. These are signs of attempts to distract from feeling. Today, consider the distractions you've been using and what they may be covering up; then, meet your discovery with compassion.

March 4

There are many things that we are afraid to let go of…
people and circumstances that we never want to leave
behind. Today, keep in mind that letting go isn't just
about endings, but about beginnings as well. In this
moment, acknowledge the necessary losses to welcome
tremendous gains and ask yourself, "Today, what is it time
to let go of and what am I willing to gain in its place?"

March 5

No matter what you have or haven't done, feelings of excessive guilt only create more of the same energy and will likely lead you to do more of the same. If you are truly ready to move forward, acknowledge your mistakes and then forgive yourself today...

March 6

Have you ever been in a crowded room and still felt lonely? We rarely heal loneliness externally—fulfillment is an internal job. What do you like about yourself today? Perhaps you'll schedule a date with yourself that is as fulfilling as being with someone else.

March 7

Try laughing today when you experience frustration. Did you know that it's actually physiologically impossible to feel as angry when you genuinely smile? When we change our physiology, we change our mood. This doesn't mean ignoring our genuine feelings. However, it does invite us to discover how we can welcome a shift when we'd like one.

March 8

How often do we judge our tears and wipe them away before they have a chance to carry us some place better? Give yourself permission to be human today; feel without judgment or justification.

March 9

Let Mother Nature teach you today. Just like the calm that comes after a storm, remember to move *with* the ebbs and flows of your emotions instead of against them and have faith that this too will pass...

March 10

Sometimes we miss out on the experience of joy because we are so focused on the door that's leaking frustrations, fears, and worries. Today, treat yourself and embark on a journey to discover the happiness in hidden places.

March 11

If you think about what evokes your anxiety, you will see that it's almost always when you are worrying about something that has already happened or something that may or may not happen in the future. Anxiety exists when our mind is visiting the past or future. For today, bring yourself to the present moment and just breathe…anxiety struggles to live in the here and now.

March 12

Be mindful of how you're talking to yourself today and
see if you can work to differentiate shame and guilt.
Guilt helps you take accountability and make changes;
it says, "I did something bad." In contrast, shame keeps
you stuck on a never ending hamster wheel of lack; it
says, "I'm bad." Where will you choose to live today?

March 13

Sometimes we say we want to move forward, but we keep one foot on the brakes. In order to be free, you must be willing to learn to let go. Release the hurt, the fear, and the hope that the past could have been any different than how it was. Welcome in old hurts and process them from a present-day perspective. The energy it takes to hang onto the past is holding you back from your present life. What are you ready to let go of today?

March 14

Are you living in "Scare-City?" How often do we allow our fears of not having enough to keep us from welcoming more? Next time you catch yourself saying, "I don't have enough," whether it is time, money, love, health, or some other driving force, notice this as fear and then shift your focus to what you do have. When you move out of Scare-City, you will move from scarcity to abundance.

March 15

Pay attention to your self-talk today. As much as we might like to believe that our symptoms of depression and anxiety have nothing to do with the way that we talk to ourselves, there is absolutely a connection. Allow your symptoms to be a road map back to your thoughts, and see what you can shift to welcome more peace today and always.

<u>March 16</u>

Feelings are never as painful as the resistance we put up against them. For today, consider allowing your feelings to flow freely instead of judging them, and notice the shift in intensity.

March 17

We spend so much energy wishing things away that we often miss opportunities to enjoy the moment. Just for today, give yourself permission to be present in each experience, and see how much more energy you have to laugh and love!

March 18

How does your fear of imperfection keep you stuck? Today, set your sights on giving things the good ole' human effort and give yourself credit just for trying!

March 19

Allow yourself to laugh with wild abandon today! When's the last time you really welcomed a good hearty belly laugh? Not a timid chuckle…a laugh so intense you've got tears streaming down your face, your cheeks are sore, and your belly is tight. If you're ready for a glimpse of your authentic self, look for the humor in your day and don't be afraid to laugh out loud!

March 20

How are goodbyes one of our wisest teachers? When transitions present themselves, allow yourself to reflect on all the treasures, grieve the loss, and celebrate the wonderfulness that you're making space for ahead. People, places, and things can always live on in our hearts, so is it ever really goodbye anyway?

March 21

Fear often keeps us from living our best life. Today, complete the sentence, "If I knew I'd succeed, I would..."

Allow your response to offer insight into the ways that fear is keeping you stuck, and then give yourself permission to take steps to move forward.

March 22

The skill of grieving doesn't just include the death of a loved one. Grieving is an important ritual that also honors what was and creates space for what will be. Whether it's the "loss" of your 30's as you turn 40, the "loss" of your kids as they grow up, or the "loss" of a reality you've gotten an updated perspective on, honor each experience and give yourself time to grieve so that you can smoothly transition to the next phase of your incredible life!

<u>March 23</u>

Get in the now. Life is simply a collection of a bunch of "nows," yet we're often so busy in yesterday and tomorrow that we miss today. When you catch yourself in the hustle and bustle today, take a deep breath and notice what is in the present.

March 24

How often do we say "I'm sorry" when we have a feeling?
If others struggle to tolerate your emotions, then that is
not your problem; it's theirs. We don't transform ourselves
by stifling our feelings; we transform by honoring them
and letting them out. So for today, embrace the motto,
"Better out than in," and let those feelings flow!

March 25

When someone gives you feedback, you often feel your stomach
drop or tighten, you want to defend yourself and lash out,
or you want to isolate and hide in shame. Instead, consider
this an opportunity to turn inward and take care of you.
What does this part of you that is reacting to someone else's
opinion need from you? What a blessing to meet the part of
you that is still in need of your love, support, and attention.

March 26

For today, how about you choose to release yourself from the feeling of not being good enough for no reason other than the fact that you're a human being and are doing the best you can! Go ahead, freedom is just a choice away...

March 27

What if you allowed yourself to see your imperfections as part of the whole? Ego believes you're either perfect OR flawed, happy OR sad, smart OR stupid…the truth is that you are a complex being with the ability to hold more than one truth at a time. Just for today, try replacing those "ORs" with "ANDs," see what shifts, and embrace your perfectly imperfect self!

March 28

Letting go hurts less than trying to hold onto something that's gone (or was never there to begin with). What are you desperately clinging to that is causing you pain? A relationship? A job? A belief? A habit? Feeling the grief of releasing is often much gentler and more manageable than our fear is telling us. Where can you get real to heal today about how you're keeping a tight grip on something it's time to release?

March 29

Feelings are our soul's way of communicating with us. Unprocessed feelings contribute to emotional and physical distress. What feelings have you been suppressing that may be showing up elsewhere in your life? For example, in that nagging back pain or persistent headache, or maybe those panic attacks or depressive episodes? Give yourself permission to release old feelings today and welcome a return to wellness.

<u>March 30</u>

For today, put the content aside and FEEL your
way through the day without judgment. Notice
what comes up and awaken to your truth.

March 31

What have you been imprisoning yourself for? You see, when we feel stuck, it's not someone else that holds the key to those prison doors we feel caught behind. You hold the key to release yourself, and it comes in the form of awareness of what thought or belief is causing you to keep yourself imprisoned. Today, examine what you're allowing to keep you stuck, and choose to give yourself permission to be free.

Chapter 4

Intention and Manifestation

As the vibration of our planet Mother Earth shifts, our ability to bring that which we desire into our life is rapidly evolving. We are co-creators of our reality. We work together with a universal energy, (some call it God, and others Buddha, Krishna, Universe, Nature, Love…no matter the name, it's all the same), to bring that which we desire into being. The challenge is that experiences of our past often leave us questioning our power and right to shine so brightly. It is when we clear our beliefs of unworthiness and reconnect with our birthrights of love, peace, abundance, and joy that we can tap into an unfathomable well of potential! As we move into April, the chapter ahead invites you on a mindful journey of exploring the ways that your thoughts and feelings can impact your life and offers specific guidance on how to make conscious that which you may be allowing to keep you from accessing your Divine reality. Here's to remembering your spiritual nature that makes you capable of designing the life of your dreams…

<u>April 1</u>

What if you knew that everything was coming together perfectly even though at times it looks as if some things are falling apart? When we trust in the process of life, it invites a calmness and an ability to live in each present moment with less fear. How would your life shift if you intentionally considered this possibility today?

<u>April 2</u>

Some people say they'll believe it when they see it, while others say they'll see it when they believe it. What do you want in your life that you've been struggling to attain? More abundance, more health, more peace, more love? Whatever it is…for today, put your energy in believing it's already on its way to you and watch what happens. You may just be pleasantly surprised!

<u>April 3</u>

Too often we allow our lack of clarity to stop us from moving forward. Today, identify the things you don't want so you can get clearer about the things that you do and use that as a guide to get clearer about your desires. No better day than today to get started!

April 4

Give yourself permission to choose an affirmation to work with today. Choose something that resonates with you at the present time since unbelievable affirmations tend to keep us stuck. For example, if you are working on body image, you might say, "I am learning to accept myself just as I am," instead of starting with, "I love my body." This is called an "in- process" affirmation and is a gentle way to meet yourself where you are and welcome you to move forward.

April 5

Dream Big! Let yourself daydream today of the wonderfulness that is in your near future. Whether this be your dream job, dream relationship, dream home, or some other dream, it's not your job to know "how"; it's just your job to picture the "what" to place the order with the Divine so the co-creation of your reality can manifest!

<u>April 6</u>

Pay attention to the ideas that are crossing your mind right now. Whether it's to quit your job and be a stay-at-home parent, start a business, or change the world, honor these thoughts as possibilities no matter how outlandish they may seem. As you sit with your ideas (which are often your soul's way of communicating to you), you become aligned with your passion and purpose and anything is possible!

April 7

Make room for something new today. This may mean cleaning out your closet, going through a pile you've been meaning to clear for a while, or even visiting a belief that no longer serves you…releasing the old allows the universal energy to know that you're ready to welcome something new. Give yourself that gift today!

April 8

How often do we stifle ourselves because we cannot yet see the end result? Are you willing to trust yourself enough to just take the next step? The only thing between you and bliss is a belief…"I can" or "I can't," "I will" or "I won't"…you choose!

April 9

What you think about, you bring about. When we spend our time and energy thinking about what's "wrong" and "bad" in our lives, we miss the opportunity to spend our time and energy creating what feels "right" and "good." Today, when you notice your mind visiting the "what if's" and the potential catastrophes, acknowledge the fear and then balance it with something you're grateful for…notice the shift.

April 10

When you go to a restaurant and order a salad, what do you expect the server to bring you? A salad, right? In order for the Divine to bring you what you want, you have to make sure you've placed the correct order. Consider creating a vision board today to depict the life you desire; use words and pictures to see your dream life on paper so that it can manifest into reality!

April 11

It is only your ego that knows limits and lack. Your Divine Self knows the truths of abundance, love, and peace. Go ahead! Imagine all of the things that you are ready to receive into your life now...and so it is!

April 12

Sometimes it is time to stop, take a deep breath, and reevaluate if you're putting your energy in the direction of making your wishes come true or in a story that they never will. Check in with yourself today and see what direction you're headed. Re-route as necessary.

April 13

What seems like it is in your way right now? Acknowledge it, take a deep cleansing breath, and choose to find the opportunity amidst the challenge. If we allow every obstacle to get in our way, we won't ever reach our destination…go ahead, think around the obstacles today!

April 14

You see, "winning" is simply a state of mind. You must "win" in your mind before you can "win" in your life. Are you thinking "winning" thoughts? Do you know without a doubt that you can "win" at whatever it is you're shooting for?

April 15

Do you have a morning routine that sets you up for a grounded and peaceful day? Maybe you'll consider waking up to music that soothes yet energizes you or spend a few moments to breathe into your day and establish your intention and plan ahead to create time for a well-balanced nutritious breakfast. Add something to your morning routine that supports you in living your best life and see what you notice!

April 16

It is rare that urgency is required in making decisions and handling our daily affairs. Can you hear parts of you screaming in disagreement!? Most of the time the urgency we feel telling us to do something immediately is just there to distract us from the feelings we'd feel if we did nothing other than breathe through the moment. Today, consider choosing to be mindful of the urgency you're giving to non-urgent matters (more than 99% of them), and just breathe your way through the day, being present with what you feel...

April 17

What do you want in your life? Step 1) Name your desire. Although you may be inclined to put an object or person in this space, identifying the feeling you'd experience when you have that thing is more likely to be successful since the Divine has access to many more possibilities than we can even imagine, and we limit ourselves when we get too specific in this way. Step 2) Believe that you deserve it. Step 3) Be open to receiving your desires.

April 18

Today, establish an intention of things going the way you'd like them to go. When you find your ego trying to dissuade you, redirect your attention to your intention. You may be pleasantly surprised by the results!

<u>April 19</u>

Come into integrity today. Take an inventory of where you are out of balance with your values. For example, if you say you value health but are eating fast food excessively or skipping meals, then you are out of congruence with that value. Today, choose one action you can shift to support you in realigning.

April 20

After your busy days, it's helpful to be intentional about rest.
Tonight, be conscious of how you are creating peace and calm
in your environment, your mind, and your body before bed.
Pay attention to what you eat, drink, watch on television, read,
and/or listen to in the evening...all of these factors can impact
mood and alter your vibration. Creating comforting bedtime
rituals can help increase the likelihood of restful sleep.

April 21

Set your intention on learning from an unexpected source today. Welcome learning from your children, parents, friends, colleagues, partners, siblings, and most importantly, those you struggle to connect with...we are both the teacher and the student; get curious today about what lesson life has in store for you, and let those around you bring it to your attention.

April 22

Whether it is some form of structured personal growth like psychotherapy or some other form of intentional transformation, give yourself permission to journey inward on purpose today. It's this conscious living that opens us up to a fabulous present and future!

April 23

If all obstacles were removed, what would you be doing differently in your life right now? Would you go back to school? Switch careers? Quit your job? Leave a relationship? Spend more time with your loved ones? Our mind is our greatest obstacle. Give yourself permission to release the illusion of "stuckness" today and claim your right to live the life you've only allowed yourself to dream of!

April 24

Choose a word or phrase in the morning and allow it to set your intention for the day. Then, in the evening, revisit your intention and see how it manifested into reality. You can use the sentence, "Today I intend to have a day filled with…"

April 25

What will you see today…opportunities
or obstacles? Your choice.

April 26

If you ordered a new couch for your living room, what would you do with the old one if the new one was scheduled to be delivered today? Most people would clear the space and make room for it, right? When you keep things that no longer serve you, it takes up the space of something that is waiting to arrive. Today, consider what you're holding onto that it's time to release so something amazing can show up.

<u>April 27</u>

Water is one of the most healing elements…rain, showers, baths, the ocean, streams, rivers, lakes, ponds, tears, fountains…when you encounter water today, honor its power to heal and intend for it to carry away that which no longer serves you so you can welcome what you now desire in that place.

April 28

What beliefs, attitudes, and/or assumptions are getting in the way of the life you imagine for yourself? It may be time to clean your mental house. Take an inventory of beliefs that are limiting your potential and consider shifting to something more expansive and allowing. Your life is waiting for you!

April 29

We send mixed messages to the Divine when we say we want one thing but hold onto another contradicting thing. For example, you say you "want" a better job, but you refuse to leave the one you have; you say you "want" a better marriage, but you're waiting for your partner to make the change. Where could you be sabotaging the potential for something new with this kind of pattern?

<u>April 30</u>

Your thoughts are more powerful than you may realize. Notice your self- limiting beliefs and challenge yourself to correct them so you can make your dreams a reality!

Chapter 5

Relationships

We experience our greatest joy and struggle in the context of relationships. We are often so desperate for being seen, heard, and loved that we engage with others in ways that leave us feeling depleted and hungry for more in our attempts to get these needs met. The truth is that the greatest relationship we ever cultivate is the one with ourselves, and yet so much of our time and energy is spent outside of ourselves trying to cajole and convince others to love us the way we crave being loved. This month we focus on ways to engage healthily in relationships while working to strike a balance between the maintenance of ourselves and our connection with others. Lean into any resistance you may notice as you read ahead into May...there are some mind-blowing concepts introduced that, if embraced, have the potential to transform your relationships to heights you have never imagined!

May 1

Love is meeting one another where we are without the need for either to be different. When we reach a place where we can be in relationship without expectation of change or attempts to control, we experience a kind of love that transcends the limits of our physical reality.

May 2

Assumptions are often the only things that stand between you and the people in your lives. Give yourself permission to check out your assumptions today. Choose a kinder, more compassionate story to narrate your reality. Human pain is created by what we tell ourselves about what happens or doesn't happen in our lives…why not write a new script if the one you are currently acting out isn't working for you? Remember today that you are the writer, director, producer, and actor in your life!

May 3

What sustains you in your closest relationships? We all
speak a different language of love. When we're feeling
unsatisfied in a relationship, it's often because we're expecting
someone to know what we want, and quite simply, they
don't. Today, go inward and discover how you most like
to receive love. Is it through words? Touch? Time? Gifts?
Share your discovery with someone you care about.

May 4

Sometimes the best way to love someone is to help them help themselves. Next time you decide that someone couldn't possibly survive without your opinion or that caretaking behavior you are itching to perform, take a deep breath and remind yourself that you wouldn't help a marathoner by running the race for them...you'd cheer them on from the sidelines and meet them at the finish line with some snacks and a hug!

May 5

Some people in our lives are better loved from afar. Contrary to popular belief, love can have boundaries, and healthy relationships function smoother because of them. Today, consider taking a relationship inventory. Who have you been keeping in your life against your higher wisdom that it may be time to consider loving from a distance?

May 6

Imagine the freedom you would experience as you release your distraction of trying to control others and remain focused on your own thoughts, beliefs, and choices? What would your relationships be like if you stopped trying to control others' feelings and behaviors and just got clear about yourself instead? Here's to your relationship liberation!

May 7

"No" is a complete sentence. Setting boundaries and limits to take care of yourself does not need to include any long or tedious justification. When you are uninterested in doing something that someone requests of you, it's as simple as saying "No" or "No, thank you." Once you move past the fear and guilt of choosing you, you'll feel the relief. Maybe an opportunity to practice this will come up today!

May 8

Let your eyes light up when your loved ones walk in the room today. We all crave being seen and heard. While we are not responsible for meeting this need for others, we can remove our own blocks to intimacy and allow ourselves to be truly present in our relationships today by really allowing ourselves to "see" someone.

May 9

People will be who they are and do what they do until they decide to be or do something different. Relationship conflict often stems from trying to change one another when we aren't ready to change. If you request change from your partner and it doesn't happen, instead of continuing to push for change, see if you can meet yourself in that reality and decide what you want to do to take care of yourself accordingly.

May 10

Contrary to common belief, abandoning our own needs to accommodate others just costs our relationships, and we pay for it later when we become angry, bitter, and resentful for doing something we didn't want to do in the first place. Taking care of YOU always helps you respect and honor the relationships you're in because you can show up most authentically and fully when you're nurtured yourself. How much self-care can you stand today?

May 11

Pay attention to who you are surrounded by at this time in your life. Since the people in our lives offer us a reflection of parts of ourselves, our relationships can help us to learn and evolve forward. Today, look for themes in your relationships…is there a lot of anger, fear, peace, sadness, jealousy, or joy around you? Be curious about how these themes may be a reflection of something it can be time for you to work on within yourself today.

<u>May 12</u>

When you meet someone whose soul is not aligned with yours, you can send them love and move along. This idea and the action of implementing it may feel "judgmental" or "mean"; however, boundary setting is one of the kindest and most loving things we can do in our relationships and encounters with one another. Judgment is saying, "I'm better than you," while love says, "We're different and I accept that." Today, if a relationship doesn't resonate with you, honor yourself and the other by acknowledging so and moving forward with love.

May 13

Everyone has a story. How would you react differently if you knew that "jerk" who just cut you off in traffic just got the news that a loved one died or that the store clerk with a bad attitude has a child sick at home that she's sad she couldn't afford to stay home from work to comfort? We're all just doing the best we can at any given moment. How can you relate to others in a human to human way today?

May 14

Ask questions today. How often do we leave ourselves to wonder and assume what a loved one meant by a word or action and sit with it alone feeling badly? Just for today, give yourself permission to check out your assumptions and ask for clarification, or at least refuse to beat yourself up with your worst-case scenario fantasy if you're not ready to check it out with your loved one yet.

<u>May 15</u>

When we judge harshly, we behave harshly. Today, choose to be conscious of the way you are judging yourself and others so you welcome loving and compassionate actions.

<u>May 16</u>

Are you a caregiver extraordinaire? Do you anticipate others' needs before they even can? We often disguise our desire for love and a sense of control in "caretaking behaviors" since when we're so focused on others' needs, we don't feel as out of control in our own. What would your life be like today if you trusted other adults to take care of themselves so that you could focus on taking care of you?

May 17

Isn't it interesting what happens in relationships when YOU change? If someone you're in a relationship with isn't willing to change, remember that you're always in control of yourself and your ability to change. When one person changes, it shifts the whole dynamic that exists…only our thoughts and beliefs trap us in unfulfilling experiences. If change is so easy…why don't YOU be the one to start today?

May 18

Just for today, get back into your own business and out of everybody else's. While we often disguise being in others' business as "helping," it's usually just a distraction from what's going on within ourselves. Sometimes, when we're feeling unsatisfied, we discover that it's because we're so busy in everyone else's affairs that no one is home managing our own. If you're so busy in everybody else's lives judging, trying to fix and control, who's running yours?

May 19

When we say "yes" and mean "no" and then hate others later, that isn't loving; that's manipulation and fear. Today, consider honoring yourself so that you can love others more. Wow, is this a shift back to a compassionate reality or what!? Dare to be "selfish" today...after all, it's truly the kindest thing you can do in your relationships.

May 20

Our greatest human desire is to be seen, understood, and
unconditionally loved…when we see people as their "roles,"
we miss their "souls" and the opportunity to truly connect.
See if you can be conscious of your connections today and be
present with your loved ones in ways that transcend your roles.

May 21

We often confuse love with fear. Love has no need to change, control, or manipulate—it simply honors what is. Fear, on the other hand, needs change and control; therefore, it tries to manipulate. Today, notice when you are "in love" and when you are "in fear."

May 22

Imagine the freedom you can experience as you release your distraction of trying to control others and remain focused on your own thoughts, beliefs, and choices. What would your relationships be like if you stopped trying to control others' feelings and behaviors and just got clear about your own feelings and behaviors? Back home to you, today...

May 23

When we feel inclined to say, "You're pushing my buttons," it lets us know that there's something in us that is unresolved and still needs healing. People can only "push our buttons" when there are buttons to push. Just for today, let these moments be your wisest teachers…be curious about what needs healing in you as you feel activated intensely in your relationships.

May 24

Take an inventory of your friendships today. Do you have a friend you perceive to be ahead of you? Beside you? Behind you? Do you have more of one kind or another? Ask yourself which is more or less satisfying and get curious about why. We are all at different points on our evolutionary journey. Release relationships that no longer resonate with you, and make room for others that will. Is it time?

May 25

Have you ever taken a risk and expressed vulnerability in
a relationship only to find that your worst-case scenario
didn't come true? Remember that time today. Staying in
our comfort zone in our relationships may feel comfortable
at first, yet it costs us true intimacy and connection.
Here's to digging in and finding your courage to show
up fully and completely in your relationships today.

May 26

Our definitions of love are often skewed. Love doesn't mean an absence of boundaries or self-care. It means, "I love us both enough to take care of myself so I do not resent you and disconnect later." Where can we truly love more in this way today?

May 27

We are such fascinating creatures, aren't we? We each participate in this delicate dance of being impacted and influenced by each other, but also taking accountability for our reactions to others' actions. Today, when you find yourself inclined to blame someone for your reaction to their action, i.e., "YOU made me feel _____," take a deep cleansing breath and take ownership of your reaction and instead communicate, i.e., "When I heard you say _____, I felt _____." Practicing this way of communicating helps to keep our relationships clean and clear and we remain empowered.

May 28

Self-assessment time! Do you trust yourself enough to surround yourself with people who will get real with you when the shadow parts of your personality emerge? Are you choosing to welcome relationships where you are gently and lovingly held accountable for your moments of insanity, relationships where you allow yourself to be harshly judged and criticized, or relationships that are so passive they do not allow you to grow? Notice your answer and make shifts according to your readiness.

May 29

We often talk about "trust" in relationships. The challenge is that when we put our trust in someone else, we are out of our realm of power and control, and we're often left blaming because we gave someone else responsibility for something that is ours. The one thing that is certain is that people will be who they are, doing what they are going to do 100% of the time. Today, focus on how you can trust yourself to cope with whatever you may or may not experience in relationship to others. Strive for self-trust!

May 30

When we can sit with one another in a state of vulnerability without the need to fix or save one another, this is love. Today, consider taking the risk of listening and relating, rather than fixing and saving...this is perhaps the most equally terrifying and liberating experience we can have in one moment!

May 31

No matter the question, Love is the answer. When we create stories and excuses as to why we can't love ourselves, we abandon our birthright of fulfillment and joy. When questions or seeming dilemmas arise today, think of what would welcome more feelings of love within you and choose that.

Chapter 6

Healing Approval Addiction

When we think of "addiction," I imagine that our minds generally gravitate towards substance abuse, right? Well I am going out on a limb here to suggest that in reality, our most popular human addiction is actually to approval. Most of us hate to admit to ourselves that we have been relying on others to make us feel special and important because we think it makes us sound weak, needy, or vulnerable. To remain in denial, we spend all this time pretending that we are secure with ourselves, that we don't care what others think, and yet when we dig deep, low and behold, we discover that one of our greatest fears is not being liked or approved of by others. It is this fear that puts the cycle of approval addiction into motion. As this cycle gains momentum over time, we begin selling ourselves out in exchange for attempting to gain the approval and validation of others. At first this may bring us comfort or an escape from an emotion (just like a drug), but eventually the costs catch up to us and we are left feeling angry, resentful, and lost as we have abandoned our Divine essence. The goal is to identify our approval addiction cycle and learn ways to tolerate our emotions long enough to be able to discover how to love and approve of ourselves so we don't consistently feel neglected as we rely on others to meet this need. After all, loving and approving of ourselves is no one's job but our own. When we take ownership of this role, our relationships become richer and more genuine, and our lives have the opportunity to flourish.

In this chapter, you will journey into the overt and covert ways your addiction to approval may be wreaking havoc in your life and explore ways to use this awareness to settle into a secure self-acceptance that puts you back in the driver's seat of your life. May you embrace your inner approval addict and give that part of you the love and approval he/she desires!

June 1

Approval of yourself is your job, not someone else's. Are you showing up for work today?

June 2

Who have you been relying on for approval of who
you are, what you do or don't do, what you say
or don't say, how you look, etc.? If the answer is
anyone other than YOU, it's time for a shift.

June 3

When we wait for others to approve of us, we give
our power away. Dare you stand in your power
and start approving of yourself today?

June 4

Ask yourself, "If I knew that everyone in my life would be absolutely thrilled with my decision, what would I do?" This question can bring you from confusion to clarity in an instant and shows you where you have been imprisoning yourself by fear of what others think.

June 5

When we make decisions based on what other people
think in order to avoid disapproval, we abandon ourselves.
Consider for a moment, how your life would change
if you could tolerate the disapproval of others.

June 6

Filter others' opinions today. When people share their opinions with us, we're often quick to either reject them quickly or accept their truth as our own. Today, instead of doing either, just notice your reaction to hearing someone else's opinion. You're beautiful. How does that opinion sit with you?

<u>June 7</u>

Life isn't about working as hard as we can to avoid disappointing others. The truth is that people may experience feelings of disappointment when we do or don't do something they wish we had or hadn't, and they have a right to feel that way. It's your job to learn to cope with the reality that others will not be pleased by every decision you make and that this is OK Can you feel your heartbeat quickening at this thought? Deep breath…

<u>June 8</u>

When we struggle to know ourselves, we let others tell
us who we are, and we believe them. When we know
ourselves, we are able to filter others' opinions and
just keep our truth. Welcome home to you, today!

June 9

Next time someone gives you their opinion, consider saying, "Thank you for sharing that perspective. I'll check in and see if that resonates with me."

June 10

What is seeking the approval of others costing you right now?

June 11

How does seeking the approval of others serve you? We only maintain behaviors that give us a gain. Maybe bending over backwards and abandoning yourself for others' approval gives you a sense of self-worth and value. Is there another way to generate a sense of worth and value that doesn't cost so much?

June 12

Before you accept something as your truth, give
yourself permission to question it and investigate
it. Only the path of YOUR truth will be joyous
and fulfilling. Whose path are you following?

June 13

Approval addiction is often an unconscious pattern that we maintain in an attempt to avoid uncomfortable feelings. Today, become conscious of when you agree to something that doesn't resonate with you and imagine what it would be like to only say "Yes" to that which resonates. Scary, huh? It's ok…they're just feelings. It's the thoughts you have about not being able to survive them that is so unbearable.

June 14

Question: Don't we have to sacrifice ourselves for others sometimes? Answer: Only if you want to live in relationships filled with resentment. While it might sound like a brave act, self-sacrifice is actually based in fear and a deep need for love and acceptance. When we love and approve of ourselves, we discover the courage to tell the truth, even if others won't approve.

June 15

Are you craving approval? Do you desperately want to be thought of as worthy, lovable, and valuable? Good news…you can start knowing these truths about yourself at any time! Why wait for others to approve of you when you have the power to do that right now?

<u>June 16</u>

Too often we make decisions based on what others want for us, and we find ourselves bitter and resentful. This is likely one of the hardest parts of growing up…choosing to live our own lives in our own way. Are you ready to put on your grown-up pants today and live the life you desire?

June 17

If you're waiting for others to approve before you choose yourself and live in a way that resonates with you, you'll probably be waiting for a while. Are you OK with that?

June 18

Question: What will people think if I _____?

Answer: What will YOU think if you _____?

June 19

Have you ever felt embarrassed by a loved one's behavior?
For example, you're at the grocery store and your child
is screaming like a wild animal in the checkout line or
your partner gets angry and yells at the server at dinner...
what have you decided it says about you that this person
is behaving in such a way? When we feel comfortable
and approve of ourselves, we are better able to let others
approve or disapprove of themselves; that's not our job.

June 20

When we need others to approve of us, we are often willing to be someone inauthentic. How are you giving others the power to define you?

June 21

The need for others to think or act a certain way in relation to us is often a sign that we're giving others control of our sense of self-worth. Today let's notice where we fear judgment and meet that part of ourselves with love to welcome more space for self-acceptance.

June 22

If you need others to approve of you, that just helps
you to know that you aren't approving of you. How
can you be more affirming of yourself today?

June 23

Confusion is often just a conflict between pleasing others or pleasing ourselves. Next time you find yourself feeling "confused," see if you can ask yourself what you would do if you knew others would approve. If this question brings clarity, then the next step is to consider your willingness to tolerate the possibility of others' disapproval.

June 24

Tolerating others' disapproval can be a painful learning process, and it's ok if you're not there yet. Just meet yourself wherever you are with love. The good news is at least you have arrived back at your truth…"I know what I want…I'm just not willing to do it right now because I'm afraid others won't like it." Tough realization…and yet it's liberating to take this kind of accountability in your life!

June 25

Have you met the part of you that takes responsibility for other people's reactions to you? This part usually sounds something like, "Oh I could never tell her I don't want to go to her party… she'd be so upset!" While it may be true that choosing to do what resonates honestly with you may generate feelings of discontent in others, that doesn't mean you aren't allowed to choose you; it just means you have to be willing to choose you AND allow others the right to feel how they feel about it.

June 26

Instead of taking on the labels and roles that others
have given you throughout your life, what if you decide
who YOU are and start fulfilling that reality instead?
Cramming yourself into someone else's vision of yourself
is stagnating. So go ahead…step outside of that box
and walk into your unlimited Divine potential!

June 27

Have you given yourself the stamp of approval yet today? If not, what are you waiting for?

June 28

Whose approval are you waiting for? As adults, we often still have parts of us that are waiting for our parents' approval. Our father who was never able to communicate he was proud, or our mother that we always perceived as critical. Today is the day to realize that others' inability to approve of you isn't about you; it's about them. Now exhale as you walk beyond the prison walls you've been keeping yourself in as you awaited their approval and give it to yourself instead.

June 29

Choose an affirmation to support your continued self-approval today. "I love and approve of myself even though..." or if that doesn't resonate with you, try, "I am learning to love and approve of myself even though..."

June 30

The day you can tolerate others' disapproval, is the day you step into your ultimate power. Today, will you consider moving through the discomfort of learning how to choose YOU even when others don't like it? Welcome home to your power!

Chapter 7

Own Your Life!

Did you know that many of us walk around giving our power away without even realizing it? It happens in our language, for example, when we say things like, "I HAVE to go to this ridiculous meeting," or, "SHE MADE me feel bad!" It shows up in our behaviors when we agree to do things we don't really want to do or, on the contrary, when we keep ourselves from doing things we want to do. These patterns are supported by many cultures and keep us stuck feeling victimized and out of control. When we are ready to take ownership in our lives, we have to be willing to give up our victim mentality and take accountability for the ways we have gotten ourselves where we are (this does not, however, mean taking ownership for other people's choices, behaviors, or actions toward you) and where we will go next. Notice any defensiveness, justifications, or excuses that parts of you may be throwing out right now as you read this. These voices are the very ones that support you in maintaining this passive pattern of making something outside of yourself responsible for your reality. This position can leave us feeling trapped and powerless. Is this ok with you? If not, good news…you can honor the opinions of these parts without buying into them as truth. Then, give yourself permission to remember your right and ability to choose to own your life, and move forward from a place of your Divine power.

The chapter ahead will help you get real about the places in your life where you are keeping yourself stuck and offer specific explorations for supporting you in moving forward and owning your life! Are you ready to give yourself permission to step out of fear, doubt, and victimhood and into your life? Buckle up…here it goes…

July 1

We all have light and dark aspects of ourselves. To live authentically, we must muster up the courage to shine light on the dark and learn more about what makes it tick. Then, we empower ourselves to make the changes we desire. What aspect of yourself are you ashamed of that you can shine some light on today? Here's to shining brightly!

July 2

It is our limited and often distorted thinking that is the cause of our "problems." When we are truthful and gentle with ourselves, we open a doorway to find miraculous solutions. For today, remember that there's only the illusion of a "problem," while the reality is filled with solutions.

July 3

Silence may have helped us survive our past, but silence will not save us now. As adults, it is our responsibility to use our voice to ask for what we need, to acknowledge our likes, and to honor that which isn't acceptable to us. Maybe today you will consider what you've been being quiet about that has a right to be heard and give yourself permission to use your powerful grown-up voice.

<u>July 4</u>

When you feel stuck or oppressed by a circumstance, relationship, or person, ask yourself, "How am I keeping myself here and what can I do to free myself?" Go ahead, claim your freedom!

<u>July 5</u>

How often do we RSVP "yes" and attend an argument simply because we were invited? Next time someone offers you this kind of invitation, see if you can take a deep breath and choose whether or not you want to engage. If not, simply say, "No, thank you." Welcome home to peace.

July 6

Why is it that we force ourselves to do things we don't want
to do, namely saying "Yes" when we mean "No," or vice
versa? We often talk ourselves into this myth that our life
isn't our own, that we "have to" this and "have to" that,
when the truth is that we can choose to "have to" or we
can choose the "want to." Just for today maybe you'll allow
yourself to choose what you "want to" and feel the liberation!

July 7

Sometimes opportunities for growth come from the most unexpected places. Today, be curious about how your life's teachers may show up in a disguise…the loss of a job, an illness or accident, a break up, a natural disaster, "bad news." When we allow ourselves to stay distracted in the belief that we are being punished by our circumstances, we miss out on seeing and experiencing the treasures in the darkness. Here's to the discovery of your rich treasures, no matter how they've been disguised!

July 8

Today, when you find yourself wanting others to change, consider how you can be more like what you want others to be. When we find ourselves saying, "I wish my partner could be more loving, affectionate, hard-working or that my boss would be more generous or my child would be more attentive and focused," we are powerless to control these outcomes. Your power lies in being the change you want to see. After all, if you think it's so easy to be or do all the things you're expecting of others…why don't YOU do it?

July 9

Next time someone says or does something that your ego wants to take personally, ask yourself, "what if it's not about me?" People's words and actions toward us really have little to do with us and most to do with them. Life turns a fabulous corner when we can begin to separate our identity from others' opinions of us and reconnect with our own!

July 10

Is it time for a filter change? Even though we may not have written our histories, we are responsible for writing our present and future. What are you writing today? Is there a change you'd like to make in your story to make your present more enjoyable? You've got the pencil…

July 11

Today, dig deep for the courage to admit the excuses you've been coming up with to avoid standing in your power and greatness. How often do you say things like, "I'd like to, but," "I wish I could, but," But But But… the truth is we do what we want to do when we're ready to do it. Today, OWN how and where you're keeping yourself stuck and meet yourself there with compassion.

July 12

How often do we reach a point in life and convince ourselves that there's nowhere to go from there and get ourselves all worked up? Fear is the ego's way of keeping us stuck and does not allow for passion-filled potential, ideas, and solutions to be generated. Next time you find yourself stuck in fear and doubt, remind yourself that it's rarely all OR nothing, and find the AND which will lead you to other options. For example, "I either get this job or I'll be broke and homeless" vs. "I realize not getting this job is a possibility, and if that happens, I will realign with my vision and try again."

<u>July 13</u>

Choose intentionally. The people, places, and things that you choose to occupy your time with can influence your energy and experience. You have the right to say "No" to people, places, and things that do not suit you for whatever reason. Are you taking care of yourself in this way today? Watch for any justifications or excuses…the truth is…the choice is all yours!

July 14

When we spend our time blaming others, we give our power away and lose the opportunity to learn about ourselves. Take a deep breath and investigate for a moment where you're blaming another, and get curious about what's been going on back home with you while you've been gone.

July 15

Thank goodness others are not responsible for your feelings (and vice versa)! "They" can never consistently do or be what you need, and it's when you expect this impossibility that you are left feeling disappointed, sad, and angry. Instead of expending energy today waiting for others to be what you need, what if you put on your adult britches and step into the challenge yourself? After all, if taking care of you is so easy, why aren't you doing more of it? Home sweet home…here is to your power!

July 16

Trust yourself today. Life is not about trusting others; it's about trusting yourself to have the skills, resources, and confidence to cope with whatever others do or don't do that you may perceive as hurtful. As you trust yourself, you rely less on the need to control others because you know you'll be ok either way. Oh, and the bonus is that makes more space to love one another!

July 17

We first have to discover and admit what we get out of our victim/"poor me" mentality before we can move into the right relationship with our empowerment. When we choose to remain in our victim mentality, we get to keep blaming others. When we step into our empowered place, we have the opportunity to see our contributions and make changes on our side of the fence, which is the only place we have any power. Who's side of the fence are you working from today?

July 18

Release that which no longer serves you. Today, take an
inventory of your beliefs, thoughts, values, behaviors,
relationships, and material possessions and get real with yourself
about their purpose in your life at this time. Then, consider
what you're willing to shift. This will help you make room
for that which is most authentic to you at the present time.

<u>July 19</u>

We cannot rely on others for change. If you want something different in your life, consider stepping up to the plate and taking ownership for changes you desire. It is no one's job but your own to take care of yourself. Notice any parts of you that may resist this and meet them with compassion and understanding...this holds the key to your power!

July 20

When we have intense reactions to other people's action or inaction that lead us to blaming, we give our power away. The question to ask yourself is, "How am I going to take care of myself when he or she does or doesn't do this thing I want them to so desperately do?" Blaming is an attempt to control by insinuating that someone should change or be different than how they are…we are all just being who we are wherever we are on our path, and when we meet one another there, that is love. Let's shift our focus back to ourselves today…yes! Welcome back home…

<u>July 21</u>

View the world with the curiosity of a child today. As if you are seeing things for the very first time, allow yourself to see something that's been in your life for a while with a new perspective, whether that be a family member, a habit, or a circumstance. See what you can discover when you set judgment and labels aside and just notice…you may be surprised!

July 22

Clinging to a past that doesn't let you choose? Whether it be five minutes ago, yesterday, last year, or ten years or more, our power never lives in the past; it exists in the present, in each "now" moment. When you find yourself visiting the past, acknowledge its presence, send love to the parts of you that experienced that moment, and show those parts of you what is here now. Here's to your present power!

July 23

When we believe that someone else has something that we "need," we give our power away. Just for today, imagine what it would be like to believe that it's impossible to need something you do not have. Mind blowing thought, isn't it? Just sit with it for a moment and try it on for size... your power belongs to you and you deserve to keep it!

July 24

Oh, how we distract ourselves from ourselves by focusing on others. When you notice that happening today, gently bring yourself back home to YOU.

July 25

Speak your truth today. Sometimes people say, "No one hears me." The question is, "Are you saying anything?" How often do we expect others to read our minds and meet our needs or change things to accommodate us? If you want someone to know something, it is 100% your responsibility to speak your truth about it and 100% the other person's responsibility to let you know if they are capable of honoring your request.

July 26

Is there a situation or circumstance in your life that feels unchangeable right now? Good news! You always have the opportunity to shift yourself to bring about a better reality... just for today, choose to see your reality from a different angle, change the way you're responding, or shift your thoughts to something more comforting and supportive... stop letting life control you...you can take charge!

July 27

Remember a time when you were in crisis and thought you'd never come out on the other side…then, realize the truth of how you grew through that crisis and into a new time and possibly even found some treasures along the way. As we shift our vibration from fear to love, we discover a well of infinite resources, healing, and peace…try that today.

July 28

No doubt that yesterday can affect today; however, instead
of giving it all of your power or pretending it doesn't exist,
allow yourself to process the past so that you may live
in the present while looking forward to the future.

July 29

How can we honor our transformation process as opposed to worry ourselves sick about it constantly? Am I doing enough? Am I being enough? Am I doing it right? Let's be honest, do we even remember the who's, what's, where's, or when's of the last thing we worried about? Just for today, set the worries aside and recognize all of the amazing ways you are transforming and learning from all of your experiences!

July 30

Where have you only been seeing one side of things? How
can you expand your awareness today and make room to
see more options, more possibilities, and more choices
so that you can feel freer and more empowered?

July 31

Let's use our words mindfully today. Speak to take ownership instead of blame, to promote peace instead of chaos, and to express love instead of judgment.

Chapter 8

Interconnectedness and Inner Wisdom

We are but one and all.

So long as there is pain anywhere, there is pain everywhere.

So long as I hate, you hate.

So long as I hurt, you hurt.

So long as I fear, you fear.

So long as I judge, you judge.

So long as I heal, you heal.

So long as I forgive, you forgive.

So long as I love, you love.

We are all but mirrors of one another. As we deepen our understanding of the depth of our interconnectedness, we can realize the ripple effect of our thoughts and behaviors. Like a pebble thrown in a still lake, it is not only where the pebble falls that responds, but the whole lake that rocks from the impact. We are being called to recognize our individual impacts on the planet at this time. We are watching as our financial, healthcare, government, and educational systems crumble and slowly rebuild on sturdier foundations of truth. Our collective consciousness is shifting to hold institutions and those individuals responsible for them accountable for their contributions to humanity. These global shifts and events are but mirrors of our own internal processes. Many of us are finding ourselves transitioning jobs, relationships, homes, beliefs…these changes are reflections of the alignment happening as we step into authenticity and connection with the global consciousness. It is time to step up and acknowledge ways we are each contributing to our planet's pain and ways we are contributing to its peace. We are individually responsible for the energy and behavior we bring to the collective. Where are we judging others instead of returning home to ourselves? Are we willing to look within when our ego wants so desperately to look without? This is a conscious choice that we have the opportunity to make several moments throughout any given day. Let's allow ourselves to be mindful of themes in our judgments as what we see in others is often an aspect of ourselves that is calling for our attention. Notice defensiveness and resistance since these reactions are opportunities for further exploration; perhaps we will dig deep for the courage to take a closer look in the mirror. Can we stand to realize the power and worth that our individual actions have on a greater scale? As we continue forward in these changing times, may we each dare to step into our greatness and discover the willingness to see the greatness in one another. This month we take a journey inward and celebrate the wisdom we discover there!

August 1

May we notice more opportunities to love instead of judge, to connect instead of unplug, and to hope instead of fear. As we each work to heal our own psyche, we shift the universal consciousness and raise the energy for the healing of humanity. What can you do to contribute your part in this today?

<u>August 2</u>

Pure magic happens when we allow our humanness to be witness in the loving presence of one another. Today, may you remember the power of holding a space of love for another.

<u>August 3</u>

Ahhhhh, forgiveness. We must forgive ourselves before we can forgive others. As we release our own self-judgments and find our humanness, our eyes and heart soften so that we may see the humanness in others. Today, remember that forgiveness says, "I give you back the part of our exchange that you are responsible for so that we may heal."

August 4

The world is for me or against me; same world, your choice. Today, you are called to evaluate your belief system about how you alienate yourself from others. The truth is that regardless of differences, as humans, we are far more alike than we are different. We all crave being seen, heard, and knowing that we matter. It's when we realize this that we join others from a place of "me AND you" as opposed to "me OR you." Here's to peace, love and justice for all!

<u>August 5</u>

As much as we'd like to think it's about something or someone outside of ourselves, it never is. It's always about us…what's going on with you gives you the lens to see outside. For today, shift your focus inward and see what's going on. Go ahead, deep breath…

<u>August 6</u>

Reconnect with the feminine parts of yourself today...
notice your gentleness, your compassion, your intuition,
and your calm, steady power. Be curious about the parts of
your feminine self you are most comfortable with and what
has the opportunity to expand or contract to re-balance.

August 7

Too often we rely on external inspiration and encouragement to get us through, and we forget about the wealth of strength within. Journey inward today, take a deep cleansing breath, quiet the outer noise, and listen to the whisperings of your Divine Self...

<u>August 8</u>

Be curious today. Instead of judging every thought, feeling, encounter, person, etc., just let yourself observe your experiences today and wonder why they might be showing up for you right now. You may just be surprised at how much calmer you'll feel and how much you learn and grow in this space of curiosity and observation.

August 9

Too often we rush full steam ahead without looking both ways. When you feel that urge to plow forward…take a sacred pause, breathe, look both ways, and then hold still while you hear the voice of your Divine Self, who is always there guiding you when you're willing to listen.

August 10

Dreams allow us to journey into the vastness of our psyche and gain insight that we are struggling to obtain in our waking state. Instead of thinking about dreams literally, consider bringing each person, place, object, and experience that shows up to life...ask what each element came to teach you. Consider keeping a dream journal to string together information over time.

August 11

Imagine what life would be like if you lived according to your own Divine wisdom instead of what someone else has prescribed you? Much joy and peace awaits you in this place...

August 12

When we're so busy judging things as "right" and "wrong," we miss the opportunities that exist in the gray area in between. We can all benefit from less judgment and more opportunity, right? Be curious today about what would happen in your life if you came from a place of curiosity about the opportunity rather than judgment.

<u>August 13</u>

Today you're invited to learn more about yourself as you see yourself in the mirrors of those around you. When you become irritated with someone else, acknowledge that irritation to yourself and then journey inward to see what part of you has been activated for healing.

August 14

Who are you allowing to direct your thoughts? When do you let others talk you into or out of your truth? For today, give yourself permission to create a filter for external feedback so that you may stay aligned with your inner wisdom.

<u>August 15</u>

What about your life is in need of a makeover and how can you step towards that today? Check in with yourself now... is it your relationship that needs a boost? Your job? Your attitude? Your home? Small changes can make a big difference!

August 16

When we turn inward and face our own demons, it becomes harder to judge and condemn the dark side in others. If we want an external experience, we have to welcome that experience internally first. We cannot expect peace in the world if our own inner world is chaotic. The world is our mirror...today, consider what is left unhealed within you and spend some time there in compassion, and then watch as your world reflects this shift back to you.

<u>August 17</u>

Be mindful of your humanness today. Treat yourself and others gently and compassionately in the face of perfect imperfections.

<u>August 18</u>

Remember that there are no experts outside of us on the inner journey. Give yourself permission to get quiet and go within today to strengthen your relationship with your wise, intuitive self...after all, this is your most powerful resource!

August 19

Release the excuses of work, family, and other external
stressors today. Make peace your internal priority
regardless of what's going on outside of yourself.

<u>August 20</u>

Reflect today on how you have been honoring yourself. Notice your reaction to your reflection...are you satisfied? If yes, celebrate that! If not, gently be curious about how you can honor yourself more authentically today. You deserve it!

August 21

We recognize in others that which we have in ourselves. Today, pay attention to the themes related to what you love and dislike as you see it in others. These are the discoveries that help you better understand parts of yourself that you've embraced and rejected. Here's to embracing your wholeness as you see all parts of you from a place of love!

August 22

Commit to taking a deep breath and going inward to solve your seeming dilemmas today...you may just be surprised by what you find when you don't race to an external source first.

<u>August 23</u>

Assess the road you are on today and adjust your speed
according to the conditions of each given moment.
Give yourself permission to slow down and speed
up as needed to successfully move forward.

<u>August 24</u>

Focus today on the light and love within you so that you can more clearly see it in those around you as well.

August 25

To tune into the channel that holds information about your life purpose, ask yourself, "If I had all the money I needed to survive, how would I be drawn to spend my time?" Often it's not that we don't know our purpose, but more that we allow obstacles to keep us from admitting and actualizing it out of fear. Not everyone fulfills their purpose through a career...some of our "jobs" are separate from our life purpose, while career and purpose are connected for others. Open your mind to broader possibilities for yourself today...

<u>August 26</u>

Our global consciousness is shifting to a time of greater peace with less hate and more love. Are you participating in judgment and hate or contributing to peace and love? It's easy to find excuses to judge and separate...today, how can you accept and join?

August 27

Be curious about the messages you may be getting from the universe today to help you have a better earthly experience. What happens when you believe that things in life happen FOR you instead of TO you? Now that's a more comforting place, isn't it?

August 28

Today you're called to remember your inner flame that is always burning and can provide warmth and clarity even in the darkest times. What can you do to rekindle your inner light right now?

August 29

Sometimes out of fear of judgment, we do not honor a path
that can help us learn what we are here to learn. Instead of
restricting yourself from this and that, be curious about what's
drawing you in different directions and trust that you can always
choose to come back to center if you feel you have strayed.

August 30

Mother Earth needs our loving thoughts right now. We are all influenced by the universal vibration...send a loving thought to our planet right now as this helps to raise the frequency and welcome a more peaceful experience for us all.

August 31

Too often we see each other's fear disguised as hatred or judgment, and then we hate and judge back to defend against the hurt. What would the world be like if we just kept on loving even when others were in fear? Isn't that a world you'd want to live in!?

Chapter 9

Nurture Yourself

You may notice that this is the second specifically "self-care" oriented chapter, and I don't imagine that you are surprised at my reason being that most of us are not particularly skilled at maintaining our personal wellness as a priority. When I speak of "personal wellness," I am not simply referring to exercise and nutrition. While those are certainly valuable pieces of the self-care puzzle, I use the term "self-care" as an umbrella term for the holistic perspective of wellness, which includes a harmonious balance of our physical, emotional, mental, spiritual, energetic, and relational selves. Creating a self-care plan that honors all facets of ourselves requires intention and mindfulness, along with an awareness of our worthiness to choose ourselves amidst all the other things we are including on our "to-do" lists. What are the signs that you've been ignoring yourself? For some, we become irritable, angry, and resentful in our relationships; for others we become physically ill or "dis-eased"; others notice symptoms of anxiety and depression, or some combination of any of the above. The better we know how our body, mind, and spirit asks us for nurturance, the more promptly we can show up and offer ourselves relief.

As you move into this next chapter, you're invited to engage in a deeper exploration of ways you can discover where you may be putting yourself last and how you can reconnect with your needs and work to meet them with love and compassion.

September 1

Remember that your self-talk is a choice. Are you repeating hurtful and unkind words to yourself that you may have heard from others at some point in the past? Commit to being nice to yourself today. Choose kind, gentle words...your body, mind and spirit will thank you!

<u>September 2</u>

Check your priority list. Are you on it?

September 3

If the only thing keeping you from saying or doing something is your belief about someone else's judgment, question that and remember that you are allowed to do things for you even when that isn't pleasing to others. Give others the opportunity to take care of themselves today and you may just be surprised at their ability to do so!

September 4

How can we grown and learn from our mistakes today instead of being so ashamed of our humanness that we deny them and stunt our growth? Mistakes are part of the human experience. Acknowledge your humanness by taking accountability for your actions or lack thereof and give yourself permission to grow beyond your wildest imagination!

September 5

While technology can be a wonderful way to connect us with each other, it can also serve as a distraction and way to unplug mindlessly. Check in today and consider if your use of technology is bringing you closer or further away from yourself and others.

September 6

What have you done for yourself lately? When we make ourselves a priority, our service to others is that much more valuable. Too often we have the best intentions to take care of ourselves and then someone else calls and asks if we're busy, and we sell ourselves out. *Newsflash* Appointments with yourself mean you are busy.

<u>September 7</u>

Honor your inner child today and do something playful and fun! Who says adults can't play outside or act silly or color or play paintball or dance or laugh? Just because we play sometimes doesn't make us irresponsible or lazy—it helps us to be healthy and balanced, which adds to our productivity when it's time for that.

<u>September 8</u>

A rainbow can remind us that there's something beautiful on the other side of a storm. May you remember to see the beauty around you today even if there are some clouds too.

September 9

How hard are we on ourselves about decision-making?
Judging ourselves always leaves us more vulnerable to
behaving in ways that don't serve us, and we end up
sabotaging ourselves...let's work to be gentle today
and remember that few decisions are irreversible.

September 10

When we treat ourselves with loving compassion, we will naturally welcome the same from others. If you're unhappy with the way people are treating you, turn inward and see where there is an opportunity to be more loving with yourself, then over time you'll be surprised to notice how others begin to do the same.

September 11

Can you feel the energy of the world shifting right now?
As we collectively work toward a more peaceful time
on our planet, our physical and emotional bodies will
likely need a little extra rest and relaxation. Tune into
your body and mind today. Let your discovery guide
you to the ways that you can take gentle care of you.

September 12

Most of us would be rich if we added up all the overtime we worked judging ourselves. How about putting all that extra time and energy into welcoming a wealth of self-love, self-forgiveness, and self-acceptance instead? Go ahead, love all over you!

September 13

There's just something about moving our body that awakens parts of us that have faded and soothes parts of us that need calming. Movement can heal our mind, body, and soul. When's the last time you got your body moving? Give yourself permission to turn on some music and honor your inner rhythm today!

September 14

Our bodies can be our wisest teachers if we tune into their wisdom. Bring your awareness to your physical body today. Without judgment, notice sensations that you feel throughout the day during various interactions and be curious about what they may be communicating to you. You can do this by noticing a sensation and asking yourself, "If this sensation could talk, it would want me to know…"

September 15

Why not intentionally commit to at least one act of kindness today? This includes being kind and gentle with yourself first and foremost!

September 16

How often do we mindlessly distract ourselves with "busy-ness?" Just for today, give yourself permission to find a few moments to do nothing without judgment of your worth. Breathe into the experience of doing nothing for a moment…

<u>September 17</u>

We don't have to create illness to communicate. When we resist speaking our truth, our bodies help us by developing "dis-ease," which then becomes our voice because we now believe we have an excuse to say "No." Today, let's give ourselves permission to feel well AND speak our needs and boundaries today…no excuses necessary, friends!

September 18

Sometimes we revert back to old behaviors or thought patterns. Instead of beating yourself up when that happens, go inward and consider what is still left that needs healing before the shift you desire can occur. It's amazing how much faster change can occur when we are kind to ourselves.

<u>September 19</u>

What are you doing to take care of yourself today? Make a conscious self-care plan instead of waiting to feel overwhelmed by the day and trying to hustle to find something to do then.

September 20

How often do we stifle our decision-making for fear that once we decide, we think there is no turning back? Very few decisions are permanent. Give yourself permission to change your mind today.

September 21

Do you have a nighttime ritual that supports you in acknowledging reactions to your day, releasing judgments, and preparing yourself for restful sleep? If you do, that is cause for celebration and recognition! If not, today you're invited to create an evening ritual to honor yourself in this way. This can be as simple as an intentional shower or bath, journaling, or a cup of your favorite herbal tea. Be conscious of how you unwind; sleep is a vital part of our wellness plans.

September 22

Give yourself permission to schedule time to relax regardless
of what's going on today. It's not your boss's, your partner's,
your children's, or your friend's job to give you time off,
and if you wait for that, you may be left disappointed.
Take accountability for your wellness and create the
time to retreat and replenish when you need it today.

September 23

When our lives become unbalanced, so do our bodies. We become "sick" as a reminder of that fact. Next time your body talks, listen and rebalance. What is your body saying today?

September 24

Some days we wake up feeling energized and ready to take on the day, while other days we just want to crawl back in bed and stay there for who knows how long! This is all part of the cycles and rhythms of life. Listen to your body today and be gentle with yourself, especially in these low energy times…just take a deep breath and know that every wave eventually makes its way to and from the shore.

September 25

Are you a chocolate or a vanilla kind of person? Some days it's important to just keep it light and on the surface…it's ok to come up for air after you've been down deep for a while. For today, treat yourself to something fun and sweet!

September 26

Are you listening to yourself today? Emotional symptoms like irritability, anger, and depression can all be signs that it's time to go inward and take gentle care of yourself. Let your symptoms bring you back home to what you need at this time.

September 27

What if there was no such thing as a "wrong choice?"
What if there were just "different" choices that lead down
different paths where more choices await you. Don't
you think that if you knew better, you'd do better? Meet
yourself where you are today and give yourself permission
to choose with the information you have right now.

September 28

It's important to take care of yourself by creating a schedule that supports you in balancing work, play, and relaxation so you can calmly deal with life's stressors. What will you do to create balance for yourself today?

September 29

Did you know that the muscles used to make a smile actually send a biochemical message to your nervous system to relax your fight/flight response? Next time you're feeling out of sorts, choose to pause, smile, and notice the shift. Say cheese!

September 30

Did you know that our "best" looks different every day?
Expecting the same level of functioning from yourself every
day is a setup for failure and self-judgment. Some days we
are well-rested, our body is feeling balance, our mind is
clear, and our emotions are regulated, while on other days,
well, we just feel out of balance. Work to be gentle with
yourself today despite the ebbs and flows of your "best."

Chapter 10

Encouragement

Sometimes we just need a little extra boost to get our motors running. Even with the best intentions we can allow ourselves to get sidetracked and end up off course from where we are heading. This month you'll journey through words of wisdom that can give you that jump start and put you back on track. Turn to this chapter when you need an encouraging pep talk, motivation, or inspiration.

October 1

Today, may you find peace in a world you may not always understand. May your pain be transformed into the strength you need to keep walking and face each new situation with courage and optimism.

<u>October 2</u>

Give yourself permission to acknowledge and
perhaps even enjoy the dance of life today no matter
which way you're moving. Cha-cha-cha!

<u>October 3</u>

Today, remember your choices, options, and your voice so you can stand in your power and access the freedom you deserve!

October 4

Examine the meaning you've given a circumstance in your life that you're experiencing as "stressful" and see if you can re-write that story to shift its intensity...you've got all the power here!

October 5

Are you filling your vocabulary and thus your life with "should" and "have to?" If so, consider how you can increase doing things you "want" instead of disempowering yourself. You might just be surprised at how quickly you'll be feeling free!

October 6

If you knew you would succeed, what would you do?
Today, write down the answer to this question and smile
knowing that the only thing standing between you and
your dreams are your self-limiting beliefs…pretty cool,
isn't it!? Perhaps it is a relief to know that as soon as
you release these beliefs and get out of your own way,
you'll be succeeding at all kinds of things! Go for it!

October 7

We're always so busy "doing" that sometimes we intervene when an equal or better outcome could have arisen even if we did nothing. Although we have parts of us that are desperate to act fast when a seeming opportunity arises, an action isn't always required. Today, ask yourself, "Will the world keep on spinning if I do nothing right now?"

October 8

Good news! You are always in control of solving your "problems" since they are always a matter of your perspective. The only problem we ever truly have is that we have forgotten our connection to the Divine energy that only knows solutions. When you feel disconnected from an answer you're seeking, take a deep breath and reconnect with your Divine Self for guidance.

October 9

Visiting and healing our pasts is a vital part of being able to arrive fully in the present moment. Remember today that you've already survived whatever was or wasn't back there. It's ok to look with your adult eyes and gain some new perspective…your present will thank you for it.

October 10

We remain powerless until we choose to take responsibility for our life by releasing blame and deciding to do what it takes to heal now. Come on, take your power back! That's the home of your fabulous present and potential future!

October 11

What are the treasures to be found in the things that happen in our lives that we spend so much time and energy trying to wish away? Even in the darkest moment, a glimmer of light exists if we just open our eyes and readjust our focus. Go ahead...look for it!

October 12

Take a risk today. When's the last time you consciously did something out of your comfort zone? If we always live within the space of comfort, we miss out on endless possibilities beyond!

October 13

Just put one foot in front of the other. Release worry about what lies ahead or behind. When it's time to turn, you'll know. The next step will be clearer without the weight of the past or the future on your mind. Trust yourself.

October 14

When we don't remind ourselves of our options and choices, we are a victim to our life and the people in it. When we acknowledge our choices, we are freed from victimhood and arrive at our personal power. Ready, set, go!

October 15

How can you be more loving with yourself today to begin
the process of welcoming the abundance you deserve?

October 16

Today, remember to give yourself credit where credit is due.
Notice the opportunities to celebrate your existence and all
the gifts you are contributing to the planet at this time.

October 17

Do something extra special for yourself today. No excuses or explanations…just think of a way to treat yourself like royalty!

October 18

Shift the way you see "mistakes" and allow yourself the room to grow and evolve though them. Recognize your amazing perfect self that exists even in the face of your humanness. For today, be gentle with yourself and notice how much easier it is to breathe...

October 19

Do something new today. How often do we allow ourselves to feel stuck in routines and forget that we have the power to change them? No more "I'm doing this because it's what I've always done." Today, examine your choices and pick one thing that's no longer resonating with you, and decide to step into something new instead. Go for it!

October 20

Too often we spend time beating ourselves up instead of building ourselves up. For today, choose to be gentle with yourself as you allow yourself to evolve on your journey.

October 21

When you are feeling "victimized," get curious about how you're allowing external factors to influence your internal experience...then choose something new...come on, just try it!

October 22

How can you stretch yourself today? Maybe it means expanding your thoughts about something beyond your current paradigm or literally stretching your body to welcome some increased relaxation and peace of mind. Meet yourself where you are and then trust yourself to reach beyond!

October 23

Today, may you remember the things that matter to you so that your life can continue to expand with passion and purpose.

October 24

Remember that you are not powerless over what walks through your mind. Notice the thoughts visiting you, acknowledge their presence, and gently send them on their way if you do not feel empowered in their presence.

October 25

Give yourself permission to sit with your physical symptoms today. Treat anything you notice as your dearest friend; treat it not as an enemy, but as a messenger who has come in peace to share information with you that will help you live your most authentic life. Nurture it, comfort it, love it…you might just be surprised by what you discover!

October 26

So often we keep our truth inside for fear of others not liking what we have to say. The truth is that your truth is not about or for anyone else; it's all about YOU! For today, give yourself permission to take care of you by sharing your perspective and feelings as they arise…as terrifying as this sometimes feels, there may just be some relief once you get to the other side…

October 27

Illuminate parts of yourself you've been hiding, release what you no longer need, and consciously set your intention on the seeds you're planting for your future. Let your feelings guide you as they ebb and flow and support you in washing away that which no longer serves your highest purpose.

October 28

Today, gently examine your life and opportunities for change. When you realize and harness your power to change, you remind yourself that you are in charge of your experience...how liberating!

<u>October 29</u>

Pain is simply part of the human experience…it's what we think about our pain that makes us suffer. Instead of rejecting emotional or physical pain when it shows up, what if you welcomed it in and asked what it was trying to communicate to you? Our bodies are always communicating…are you listening?

October 30

Each time you survive a bump in the road, it smoothes you out and prepares you to more easily flow through whatever lies ahead.

October 31

Wherever you are today, doing whatever you're doing, show up and make the best of it or pick somewhere or something else to do where you can.

Chapter 11

Count Your Blessings

Gratitude is the single most important practice of our lives. It welcomes a kind of peace and joy in our hearts that only grace knows. Gratitude isn't just a feeling; it is an experience that we cultivate through intentional daily practice. Intentionally practicing gratitude, even when it seems there isn't anything to be grateful for, prepares and trains you to be able to access joy and light even in the darkest of times. So even on days when gratitude is the last thing on your mind or in your heart, maybe you'll allow yourself to do your gratitude practice for a moment and see how this experience realigns you with your Divine Self.

You'll notice that the chapter ahead is different than the previous ones as it offers journaling prompts and exercises to support you in developing your daily gratitude ritual. Each day you will be progressively introduced to another aspect or step in the process of developing your practice. There is a mindfulness about gratitude that takes time to establish; it isn't simply about saying "thank you," but rather about the combination of acknowledging your blessings and feeling grateful in your heart. At first you may notice the experience more in your head…that's the value of practicing. Then, you allow the feeling to awaken in your heart as well. It's when this feeling awakens that your vibration shifts and you begin to draw more blessings into your life than you could ever dream possible! Perhaps you'll create a gratitude journal where you'll capture your gratefulness, or you may choose to write directly here in the book or copy the pages so you can use them again and again. As you move through each day this month, you may discover that some practices resonate with you more deeply than others…honor that self-awareness and continue using those; personalize this chapter to meet your needs. This month is simply an introduction; once you get your feet wet, you'll likely notice yourself in a space of pure grace naturally as you move through your days, spontaneously bursting with inspiration!

November 1

Gently close your eyes, take a deep breath, and
allow one of your blessings to come to mind.

November 2

Even though _____ , today I am thankful for...

November 3

Today, let nature be your guide. Look outside or step outside if you feel inclined, and breathe in the blessings of Mother Earth. Name one thing you see or are experiencing that you appreciate in this moment.

November 4

A person in my life I am grateful for today is…

November 5

An experience I am grateful for welcoming into my life is…

November 6

Something I didn't know how to appreciate at the time but now recognize as one of my life's greatest blessings is…

November 7

If my gratitude had a voice, I'd hear it say...

November 8

Think of something specific that someone in your life said or did that generated a sense of gratefulness in you and reminisce about that feeling now...

November 9

Before falling asleep tonight, gently allow your
eyes to fall down, take a deep cleansing breath, and
name three things you feel grateful for today.

November 10

Spontaneously list five things you feel
grateful for in this moment.

November 11

Who do you feel inspired by? Notice what happens
in your body as you allow the answer to this question
to rise to the surface of your awareness.

November 12

The color of my gratitude is…

November 13

Today I felt grateful when…

November 14

I notice that when I allow myself to
acknowledge and feel grateful...

November 15

Today, when I feel grateful, I allow myself to say it out loud.

November 16

My experience of gratefulness expands when…

November 17

If I could bottle my gratitude up and sell it
as a fragrance, it would smell like...

November 18

When I think of ___, I always smile.

November 19

The place gratitude lives in my body is…

And I know this because…

November 20

_____ felt like a curse, but I now realize
it was a blessing in disguise because...

November 21

Before my feet hit the floor in the morning, I practice gratitude.
This morning as I wake, I feel infinite gratitude for...

November 22

Think of someone you feel grateful to have in your life today and at least one specific reason why…then share it with them.

November 23

What inspires you? Feel your answer...notice
where inspiration shows up in your body.

November 24

Send a thank you note today.

November 25

If I had a picture of my gratitude, it would be of…

November 26

Spontaneously make a list of ten things you feel gratitude for...

<u>November 27</u>

In this moment, my heart is filled with gratitude about...

<u>November 28</u>

The shape of my gratitude is...

November 29

When I am willing to listen, I hear my gratitude say...

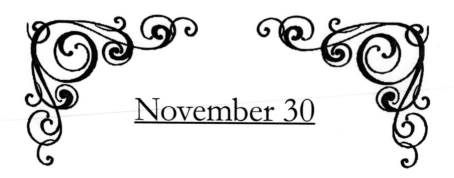

<u>November 30</u>

Since intentionally participating in a gratitude
practice this month, I notice that…

Chapter 12

Authentically You

Birthing our authentic selves, much like childbirth, can be a laborious and painful process. Yet we are each pregnant with a Divine purpose and the gifts to realize our potential. The issue is that we often allow our lights to dim as we spend years hiding our humanness behind masks of perfection, which lead us to lose the sense of our authentic selves in all the inner chaos and clutter. When we let our fear of being undesirable to others keep us from being true to ourselves, we have to pay the consequences of that choice. Over time, the cost of our avoidance of authenticity is exhaustion, depression, anxiety, and the list goes on and on. Has your debt to the bank of authenticity become more than you are willing to pay? This chapter is a daily exploration of the ways you can stretch yourself out of your comfort zone, dissolve your masks of inauthenticity and unapologetically step into the beautiful true self you actually are!

The truth is that we aren't here to be perfect. We are here to be whole. While you walk through the peaks and valleys of your human journey, may you remember to be gentle and breathe deeply and intentionally as you welcome your beautiful bundle of joy…congratulations…it's your Divine Authentic Self!

December 1

Today, you are being called to peel away layers of inauthenticity. We often build these layers over time out of fear, and now it is time to give yourself permission to admit who you really are underneath it all...not just the parts of you that are perfectly polished, but the parts of you that are struggling and raw too. You are a multi-dimensional being, and it is ALL of these aspects of yourself that make you whole...embrace all of you today!

December 2

How often do we silence our heart because we're telling ourselves the story that it isn't "convenient" or "acceptable" to let it speak? In the past we have often been directly or indirectly told to "stop feeling," but now as adults, we have to decide to let parts of ourselves feel if we want to be free. For today, see if you can acknowledge the words of your heart and welcome their wisdom…let them flow!

December 3

Reconnecting with Mother Earth is one of the quickest ways to access your most authentic self. This doesn't have to be a ten mile hike or a whole day at the beach (although it can be), but rather an intentional breath of the fresh air, listening to the chirping of the birds, or feeling the blowing of the breeze on your face as you walk to your car. What can you do to reconnect with nature and thus yourself today?

December 4

You've already survived your past. Instead of beating yourself up for what you did or didn't do back then, acknowledge the truth of your humanness and give yourself permission to love yourself in the present so that you can make your way into your abundantly beautiful future!

December 5

Say what you mean. So often we talk just to fill space and avoid silence or disapproval, and our words are dishonest and unclear. Today, bring your awareness to where you are incongruent with your words. Take a sacred pause before speaking and check in with your Divine Self about your truth, and then speak if it makes sense to do so.

December 6

Who do you give yourself permission to show your authentic self to? First we have to be willing to honor our authentic self internally, and then we can let ourselves get real with one another. As terrifying as it often feels, it's a beautiful gift when two souls allow themselves to authentically connect. Are you willing to make a genuine connection today?

<u>December 7</u>

We spend so much time in life attempting to protect
ourselves from getting hurt that we prevent ourselves
from taking a risk that may turn into a happy ending.
Find one of your walls today and start chipping…

<u>December 8</u>

How often do we stifle our song just waiting for the "right" words or answers? The truth is that you're allowed to sing even when you're still figuring out your song! You don't have to wait until you have everything just so. We're all a work in progress, and our voice is often our way to the clarity we are seeking. La La La!

December 9

As you continue to journey inward and discover your authentic self, it's important to honor the process of shedding protective layers that you've built to support you in arriving at this point.

For today, acknowledge the aspects of yourself that have gotten you to this moment and thank them for their efforts.

December 10

How much energy are you spending smiling and essentially lying to yourself and others about how you're doing? It's ok to not feel ok 100% of the time. Strangely enough, you may just find that the more honest you are about how you're doing, the more ok you'll feel. Oh, the irony! Here's to thinking and responding authentically today when someone asks, "How are you?"

December 11

What would your life be like if you created time to be with your loved ones with intention? Letting others witness your visions, hopes, and dreams can be equal parts terrifying and empowering...who are you allowing to really see you today?

December 12

What thoughts or beliefs have you attached to yourself that are not in harmony with your highest self? Today, bring your focus to a thought or belief that is not serving you and move into the vastness of the space you create and rest there.

December 13

Tell yourself the truth today—not the candy-coated version of what you want to hear, but the real deal. It is in this authentic place of rigorous honesty that healing happens, for denial just maintains our old patterns. Your evolution comes from truth!

December 14

Our ego is judgmental. Our soul is comfortable accepting the reality of what is in each present moment. Ask yourself right now, "Am I leading with Ego or Soul?"

<u>December 15</u>

Are you doing things out of habit or passion? Just because you did something yesterday doesn't mean that it will resonate with you the same way today. As you move about your day today, ask yourself this question…habit or passion? Habit or passion?

December 16

How can you be a midwife to rebirthing yourself today? Each day is a new opportunity to birth more of your authenticity and genuineness. Today, you're invited to do this with intention and love. Wishing you a swift and easy labor!

December 17

When we all walk around pretending to be "normal" and "perfect," covering up our humanness from one another, it keeps us separate and disconnected. The truth is that we are all variations of "normal." We all feel insecure, not good enough, grateful, sad, angry, happy, scared, and jealous from time to time. For today, maybe you'll consider where you can take down your mask of perfection that takes so much energy to maintain and just be human with someone instead.

December 18

Today, you are waking up with the possibility of being more authentic than you were able to be yesterday. Each day is a new change to take steps in birthing your most authentic self. What can you do today to shed another layer of inauthenticity and embrace more of your Divine Self?

December 19

The consequences of keeping your authentic self chained and boxed up are far greater than the fear of stepping into yourself. Where do you still have yourself chained down? You have the key to unlock those chains…it exists in your thoughts, beliefs, and then your actions. Look around inside yourself today. Will you set yourself free today?

December 20

Life isn't about being better than others. It's about being the best version of yourself. Maybe today you'll put away the measuring stick of comparing and contrasting yourself with those around you and turn inward to discover how you can be more of yourself.

December 21

Integrity is when your behaviors are aligned with your values. Today, visit your values and see how congruent you are being. Sometimes it's time to shift or redefine our value system as we get closer to our authentic selves, and other times we discover the opportunity to shift our behavior to realign with our values. No self-judgment, my friend! Just curiosity and love…these sentiments help change come more swiftly.

December 22

How can we live more authentically this time of year?
Are you agreeing to participate in holiday traditions
just because it's what you've always done, or are you
consciously choosing? Check in with your highest self and
see how you can honor your spirit by listening to your
heart's desire and saying "yes" and "no" accordingly.

December 23

Now is the time to let your authentic self out of the proverbial closet, my friend! Mother earth is calling on us to honor our truest selves so that we can compassionately gather to support one another through these times of intense transition on our planet. Look for one way to be true to yourself today; kindly say "no, thank you" to offers that do not stir passion in you and "yes" to those that fuel your inner flame.

December 24

Today, you're invited to distinguish between the truth of your beliefs and values and the ones you have been holding onto for others that do not resonate with you. For example, if your family of origin always held the belief that "men shouldn't show emotion," how does that opinion resonate with you now? Is that a truth that you aspire to or one that you'd like to leave with your family?

December 25

Birthing our authentic selves can be a laborious process.
The truth is you have always been worthy, fabulous,
and beautiful, even when you've forgotten. Today,
celebrate the progress you've made in birthing various
aspects of your true Divine nature into being!

December 26

As a new year approaches, take some time today to reflect on the past year. Remember moments that generated feelings of joy and peace and bask in those feelings now.

December 27

Today, evaluate how you've grown over the past
year. Give yourself credit for the ways you've
made yourself and your evolution a priority!

December 28

Today is a time for reflection of what you'd like to transcend beyond in the year to come. What are you holding onto today that no longer serves your highest purpose? In the new year, it is my intention to release...

<u>December 29</u>

A new year is almost upon you, and this is a popular time of year to be thinking about goals and resolutions. While we may have the best intentions in this process, as humans we aren't oriented to be so rigid and exact…our growth is a process that takes time, and sometimes we use resolutions to set ourselves up for failure and self-punishment. Instead, today you're invited to ask yourself, "What is it my intention to welcome into this new cycle of my life?

December 30

Today, identify at least three things you are proud of yourself for this year. Go ahead, give yourself credit where credit is due…celebrate YOU!

December 31

We can no longer get away with mediocrity in terms of our authenticity. We are being called to go deeper and deeper within each day and commit to knowing and loving ourselves in ways we haven't given ourselves permission for in the past. How will you honor yourself today and peel back yet another layer of false self to get to the genuinely delicious and fabulous you? Imagine a world with all that authenticity...pure ecstasy!

About the Author

Keri Nola is the founder of Path to Growth, LLC, a Central Florida based integrative healing center that blends traditional and holistic techniques for journeys to peace. As a Licensed Mental Health Counselor, Keri provides psychotherapy and facilitates therapeutic retreats for those seeking to reconnect with their inner wisdom, particularly after trauma or loss. In addition, she is frequently sought after to provide heart-inspired business consultation for healthcare professionals. Currently pursuing her doctoral degree in Holistic Theology, Keri is focusing her studies on ancient forms of spiritual healing. Keri lives in Orlando, Florida where she finds tranquility in spending time by the water and by painting life's inspirations.

CPSIA information can be obtained at www.ICGtesting.com
Printed in the USA
LVOW08s2345140716

496424LV00001B/16/P